MW01713397

PRINCE HARRY

THE MAKING OF A MODERN ROYALTY

JOHNSON J

ISBN:

Table of Contents

INTRODUCTION

Prince Harry, also known as His Royal Highness Prince Henry of Wales, is a member of the British Royal Family and the younger son of Prince Charles and Princess Diana. Born on September 15, 1984, Prince Harry has had a unique and often controversial life, from his early days as the mischievous younger brother of Prince William to his recent decision to step back from his royal duties.

This book aims to provide an in-depth and objective look at Prince Harry's life and impact, from his childhood and education to his charitable work and role in the Royal Family. Through an examination of his personal and public life, we will explore how Prince Harry has become a modern royal and how he continues to shape the monarchy and society. The book also aims to provide an understanding of Prince Harry's decision to step back from his royal duties and how it has changed his life and legacy.

In addition to his royal duties, Prince Harry has also been known for his charitable work and philanthropy. He has been involved in a variety of causes, including mental health, veterans' issues, and conservation. He has also been a strong advocate for social justice and has used his platform to raise awareness about issues such as poverty and inequality.

Throughout his life, Prince Harry has also had a number of high-profile relationships, but none more notable than his marriage to American actress Meghan Markle. Their relationship, courtship and marriage has been widely covered by the media, and continues to make headlines even today.

This book will delve into all these aspects of Prince Harry's life, from his childhood and education, to his royal duties and philanthropy, his relationship with Meghan Markle and family and the road to independence and his impact and legacy. It will provide an in-depth and well-rounded understanding of Prince Harry's life and how he has become a modern royal, and how he continues to shape the monarchy and society.

1

EARLY LIFE AND EDUCATION

Prince Harry, also known as His Royal Highness Prince Henry of Wales, was born on September 15, 1984, at St Mary's Hospital in Paddington, London. He is the younger son of Prince Charles and Princess Diana, and the younger brother of Prince William. Growing up, Prince Harry spent his early years living at Kensington Palace in London, and later at Highgrove House in Gloucestershire.

Prince Harry's childhood was marked by the high-profile and often tumultuous marriage of his parents, and the subsequent divorce. Despite the challenges, Prince Harry had a close relationship with his mother, Princess Diana, who was known for her warmth and compassion. She instilled in him a sense of social responsibility, which he would later carry throughout his life.

Prince Harry received his primary education at Wetherby School in London, followed by Ludgrove School in Berkshire. He later attended Eton College, where he excelled in sports, particularly rugby and polo. He also had a keen interest in art and photography.

After completing his education, Prince Harry went on to attend the Royal Military Academy Sandhurst, where he trained as an officer in the British Army. He was commissioned as a second lieutenant in the Blues and Royals regiment of the Household Cavalry in April 2006. He served in the army for 10 years, and had two tours of duty in Afghanistan. During his time in the military, Prince Harry earned the rank of captain and served in a variety of roles, including as a reconnaissance troop leader and an Apache helicopter pilot.

In this chapter, you will find a detailed account of Prince Harry's childhood, family life, education, and military training. It will delve into his early influences and how they shaped his later life and career. It will also give you a glimpse of his personality and character that he developed during his formative years.

Prince Harry's education also included an exchange program to Australia, where he spent time at a cattle station in the Northern Territory. This experience gave him an appreciation for the Australian way of life, and he would later return to the country on several occasions, including on a solo trip in 2003.

In addition to his formal education, Prince Harry also received training in various outdoor activities such as skiing, scuba diving and white-water rafting. He also developed a love for adventure and travel, which would become a recurring theme throughout his life.

Prince Harry's time at Sandhurst also shaped him as a person and a leader. He thrived in the rigorous training and discipline of the military academy, and his time in the army instilled in him a sense of duty and responsibility. He also had the opportunity to lead soldiers on operational deployments, and he was known for his dedication to his men and his leadership skills.

Furthermore, Prince Harry's time in the military also gave him a unique perspective on life and the world, as he had the opportunity to interact with people from all walks of life and see the world from different angles. He also developed a deep respect for the sacrifices made by veterans and their families, which would later become an important focus of his philanthropy.

Overall, this chapter provides a comprehensive look at Prince Harry's early life and education, and how it has shaped him into the person he is today. It covers his childhood, family, education, and military training, and highlights how these experiences have influenced his later life, career and personality.

2

ROYAL DUTIES AND RESPONSIBILITIES OF PRINCE HARRY

Prince Harry, also known as His Royal Highness Prince Henry of Wales, has a number of official duties and responsibilities as a member of the British royal family. Some of these include:

1. Representing the Queen and the royal family

at various events and engagements, both in the UK and abroad.

2. Supporting the Queen and other members of

the royal family in their official duties.

3. Promoting charitable causes and organizations, particularly those related to mental health and wellness, veterans, and conservation.

4. Participating in ceremonial events and military parades, such as Trooping the Colour and Remembrance Sunday.

5. Acting as a patron or president of various organizations and charities, including the Invictus Games, which supports wounded veterans and service members.

6. Supporting and promoting the UK's interests abroad, through visits and engagements with foreign leaders and dignitaries.

7. Participating in the monarchy's ceremonial and symbolic roles, such as the opening of parliament and the state opening of parliament.

8. Supporting the work of The Royal Foundation, which is the principal charitable and philanthropic vehicle of The Duke and Duchess of Cambridge and The Duke and Duchess of Sussex.

As Prince Harry is no longer a working member of the Royal Family, he does not have any official duties and responsibilities, he is free to pursue his own charitable and philanthropic interests.

Additionally, Prince Harry also has a number of personal interests and pursuits that he actively engages in as part of his royal duties and responsibilities. Some of these include:

1. Advocating for social and environmental issues, such as climate change and sustainable living.

2. Supporting and promoting the work of various organizations and charities related to children, youth, and education.

4. Encouraging and supporting young people to become involved in their communities and to take an active role in shaping the future.

5. Promoting cultural understanding and fostering positive relationships between different communities, both in the UK and abroad.

6. Encouraging and supporting the education and development of young people, particularly those from disadvantaged backgrounds.

7. Advocating for mental health and wellness, and working to reduce the stigma surrounding mental health issues.

8. Promoting physical fitness and healthy living through his involvement in various sports and fitness initiatives.

Using his platform as a member of the royal family to raise awareness and support for various causes and organizations, including those related to poverty, homelessness, and social inequality.

Overall, Prince Harry's duties and responsibilities as a member of the British royal family are wide-ranging and multifaceted, and are focused on promoting the values and interests of the monarchy, supporting charitable causes and organizations, and encouraging positive social and cultural change.

In addition to his official duties and responsibilities, Prince Harry also engages in a number of personal projects and initiatives that align with his interests and passions. Some of these include:

The Archewell Foundation: Prince Harry, along with his wife Meghan Markle, founded the Archewell Foundation, a non-profit organization that focuses on promoting community service, education, and the arts. The foundation also focuses on the issues of gender equality and racial justice.

Invictus Games: Prince Harry is the founder of the Invictus Games, an international adaptive sports event for wounded, injured and sick servicemen and women, both serving and veterans. The games were created to inspire recovery and support rehabilitation and provide an opportunity for servicemen and women to use sport as part of their recovery process.

Supporting the military: Prince Harry is a former Army officer and has a strong connection with the armed forces. He continues to support military veterans and their families through various initiatives and organizations.

Sustainable Tourism: Harry has been vocal about the importance of sustainable tourism and the impact of human activities on the environment. He has advocated for sustainable tourism, including responsible travel and ecotourism, as a means of protecting natural resources and supporting local communities.

Mental Health: As a patron of various mental health organizations and charities,

Prince Harry has been an advocate for mental health awareness and has spoken openly about his own struggles with mental health. He has also been actively working towards reducing the stigma surrounding mental health and promoting mental wellness.

Overall, Prince Harry has a wide range of interests and passions, and he uses his platform as a member of the royal family to promote and support various causes and organizations that align with these interests. He is also actively working towards making a positive impact on the world through his various personal projects and initiatives.

3

PRINCE HARRY'S RELATIONSHIP WITH HIS WIFE MEGHAN

Prince Harry, also known as His Royal Highness Prince Henry of Wales, met his wife Meghan Markle in 2016. They were introduced through a mutual friend, and their relationship quickly developed. They announced their engagement in November 2017 and were married in a ceremony at St. George's Chapel at Windsor Castle in May 2018.

The couple has been known for their modern and progressive approach to their roles as members of the royal family. They have been vocal about their desire to use their platform to promote various social and humanitarian causes, including gender equality, racial justice and mental health awareness.

In January 2020, the couple announced that they would be stepping back from their roles as senior members of the royal family and would be working towards becoming financially independent. They also announced their plan to split their time between the UK and North America.

In August 2020, they announced they would not return to their roles as working members of the Royal Family. They also stated that they will not be using their HRH titles anymore and will repay the Sovereign Grant expenditure for the renovation of Frogmore Cottage.

The couple has been active in various charitable endeavors, including the launch of the Archewell Foundation, an organization focused on community service, education, and the arts. The couple also continues to be active in various other charitable causes and organizations, such as the Invictus Games, which supports wounded veterans and service members.

Overall, Prince Harry and Meghan Markle have a strong and supportive relationship, and they have used their platform as members of the royal family to promote various causes and organizations that align with their shared interests and passions. They have also been vocal about their desire to live a more independent and progressive life, and have been actively working towards this goal.

In addition to their charitable work, Prince Harry and Meghan Markle have also been vocal about the importance of privacy and personal boundaries. They have spoken publicly about the pressure and scrutiny they faced as members of the royal family, and have been open about the need to protect their mental and emotional well-being.

The couple also faced a lot of criticism and media attention, specifically Meghan faced a lot of negative coverage in the press, which led to the couple suing the British press. The couple also faced some criticism from the royal family and the public for their decision to step back from their roles as senior members of the royal family.

Despite these challenges, Prince Harry and Meghan Markle have continued to support each other and to work towards their shared goals and interests. They have settled in the United States and have been actively working on various projects, including their Archewell Foundation, which aims to create a more compassionate and connected world. They are also actively using their platform to raise awareness for various causes, including racial justice and gender equality

In addition, the couple has been vocal about their plans to focus on their family, after the arrival of their son, Archie. They have been vocal about their desire to raise their child away from the public eye, and have been actively working towards creating a more private and normal life for their family.

Overall, Prince Harry and Meghan Markle's relationship is built on mutual support and shared goals. They have faced many challenges and criticism but have remained committed to their desire to live a more independent and progressive life and make a positive impact on the world through their charitable work and advocacy.

5

HARRY'S MEETING AND COURTSHIP WITH MEGHAN

Prince Harry and Meghan Markle first met in July 2016, through a mutual friend in London. The couple has described the meeting as a blind date, and they immediately hit it off. They kept their relationship private for several months, but their relationship was eventually made public in October 2016.

After a few months of dating, Prince Harry took Meghan on a romantic trip to Botswana, where they camped under the stars and spent time getting to know each other in a secluded and peaceful setting. The couple later revealed that this trip was a turning point in their relationship and solidified their feelings for each other.

As their relationship progressed, Prince Harry and Meghan Markle faced significant media attention and scrutiny. They faced criticism for their age difference and Meghan's status as a divorced, biracial actress. Despite this, the couple remained committed to each other and continued to build a strong relationship.

In November 2017, Prince Harry proposed to Meghan and they announced their engagement to the public. The couple chose a ring that featured a diamond from Botswana, a nod to their special trip together, and two smaller diamonds from his late mother's collection, Princess Diana.

The couple's engagement was met with widespread excitement and anticipation, and they were married in a ceremony at St. George's Chapel at Windsor Castle in May 2018. The ceremony was attended by family, friends and many dignitaries, and was watched by millions of people around the world.

After their wedding, the couple settled into their new roles as the Duke and Duchess of

Sussex, and began their official duties as members of the royal family. Throughout their courtship and marriage, Prince Harry and Meghan Markle have shown a deep commitment to each other and to their shared goals of making a positive impact on the world through their charitable work and advocacy.

In the months and years following their wedding, Prince Harry and Meghan Markle have been actively engaged in charitable work and advocacy, both separately and together. They have focused on issues such as mental health, gender equality, and racial justice, among others. They have also used their platform to promote various organizations and causes that align with their shared interests and passions.

The couple has also been open about the challenges they faced as members of the royal family, particularly in terms of the intense media attention and public scrutiny they received. They have been vocal about their desire to live a more private and independent life, and have been actively working towards this goal.

In January 2020, Prince Harry and Meghan Markle announced that they would be stepping back from their roles as senior members of the royal family, and would be working towards becoming financially independent. They also announced their plan to split their time between the UK and North America. This decision was met with mixed reactions and some criticism.

In August 2020, the couple announced that they would not be returning as working members of the Royal Family, and that they would not be using their HRH titles anymore. They also stated that they will be repaying the Sovereign Grant expenditure for the renovation of Frogmore Cottage.

Despite the challenges they have faced, Prince Harry and Meghan Markle have remained committed to each other and to their shared goals of making a positive impact on the world through their charitable work and advocacy. They have settled in the United States and have been actively working on various projects, including their Archewell Foundation, which aims to create a more compassionate and connected world.

Prince Harry, also known as Henry Charles Albert David, is the younger son of Prince Charles and Princess Diana. He was born on September 15, 1984, and is currently sixth in line to the British throne. Throughout his life, Prince Harry has had a close relationship with his family and has been open about the impact that the loss of his mother, Princess Diana, had on him.

In 2011, Prince Harry began dating Meghan Markle, an actress known for her role in the legal drama "Suits." The couple announced their engagement in November 2017 and were married on May 19, 2018, at St. George's Chapel in Windsor Castle. The wedding was a highly-publicized event, with millions of people around the world tuning in to watch the ceremony.

As a married couple, Prince Harry and Meghan Markle have been very active in charitable causes, particularly those related to mental health and the empowerment of women and girls. They have also been vocal about their desire to live a more private life, away from the intense media scrutiny that often comes with being a member of the royal family.

In January 2020, Prince Harry and Meghan Markle announced their decision to step back as senior members of the royal family and to become financially independent. This decision was met with mixed reactions, but the couple has made it clear that they wish to continue to support and serve the Queen and the Commonwealth.

In March 2020, Prince Harry and Meghan Markle announced that they were expecting their first child, Archie Harrison Mountbatten-Windsor, who was born on May 6, 2020. In 2021, they announced that they were expecting their second child, a girl, Lilibet Diana Mountbatten-Windsor.

The couple has also focused on building their brand, especially through their Archewell Foundation, which aims to empower and inspire communities to create a more equitable and compassionate world.

Overall, Prince Harry's family life and marriage to Meghan Markle have been marked by a desire for privacy and a dedication to charitable causes. Despite facing challenges and criticism, the couple has remained committed to each other and their family, and continues to make a positive impact in the world.

6

HARRY AND MEGHAN'S DECISION TO STEP BACK FROM ROYAL DUTIES

Prince Harry, also known as Henry Charles Albert David, is the younger son of Prince Charles and Princess Diana. He is sixth in line to the British throne. In January 2020, Prince Harry and his wife Meghan, the Duchess of Sussex, announced their decision to step back from their roles as senior members of the royal family, and to become financially independent. This decision was met with mixed reactions from the public and members of the royal family. Since then, Prince Harry and Meghan have moved to North America and have taken on various endeavors, including philanthropy, activism, and media projects.

Prince Harry has had a significant public profile from a young age, due to his royal heritage and the tragic death of his mother, Princess Diana. He has had a successful military career, serving in the British Army for over a decade and completing two tours of duty in Afghanistan. He also became known for his philanthropic work, particularly with regard to mental health, the Invictus Games, and wildlife conservation.

In addition to his military and philanthropic pursuits, Prince Harry has also been a prominent figure in the media, both in the UK and internationally. He has been involved in various charitable and humanitarian causes, and has advocated for issues such as LGBTQ+ rights, sustainable tourism, and the welfare of veterans.

Prince Harry's decision to step back from his role as a senior royal and become financially independent was a significant moment in the history of the royal family. The announcement came after months of speculation and rumors about the couple's dissatisfaction with their roles and the treatment they had received from the media. The decision was met with mixed reactions, with some supportive of the couple's desire for more privacy and autonomy, while others criticized the move as disrespectful to the royal family and damaging to the reputation of the British monarchy.

Since leaving the royal family, Prince Harry and Meghan have settled in North America and have taken on various endeavors, including philanthropy, activism, and media projects. They have also launched their own nonprofit organization, Archewell, which aims to promote "compassion, kindness and community". They signed a multi-year deal with Spotify to create and host podcasts, and with Netflix to create content for the streaming service. They also announced a partnership with Proctor & Gamble to promote racial and gender equality.

Prince Harry's move towards independence is a significant change from his previous role as a senior member of the royal family, and it remains to be seen what impact it will have on his relationship with the royal family, and on his public image and reputation.

Prince Harry's move towards independence has also brought some challenges for him and his wife Meghan. They have faced some criticism for the way they have handled their transition, particularly in regards to their financial arrangements and their communication with the royal family. They were also criticized for their decision to use their royal titles in their commercial ventures, and for their use of private jets despite promoting environmental causes.

In addition, they faced legal battles with the media over their privacy, with Meghan suing a British newspaper for publishing a letter she wrote to her father and Harry suing several media outlets over their coverage of his wife.

However, they have also received support from many people who believe they have the right to make their own choices and live their lives as they see fit. They have also continued to use their platform to promote important causes and issues, such as mental health, racial equality and women's rights.

It is worth mentioning that the couple's decision to step back from their roles as senior members of the royal family was not only driven by their desire for more privacy and autonomy, but also by their wish to financially support themselves and not rely on public funds. They have also made it clear that they want to continue to support the Queen and the royal family in their work, but in a more limited capacity.

Overall, Prince Harry's move towards independence has been a significant and complex transition, and it will be interesting to see how it unfolds in the future.

7

HARRY MOVED TO NORTH AMERICA

Harry, a young professional in his late twenties, moved to North America in search of new opportunities and experiences. He had always been drawn to the vibrant and diverse culture of the continent, and was excited to finally make the move.

Upon arrival, Harry settled in a bustling city on the East Coast. He quickly found a job in his field of expertise and began to immerse himself in the local community. He volunteered at a local non-profit organization, joined a sports league, and made new friends from all walks of life.

Despite the initial challenges of adjusting to a new country and culture, Harry thrived in his new environment. He was able to advance quickly in his career and was recognized for his hard work and dedication. In addition to his professional success, Harry also had the opportunity to travel extensively throughout North America, visiting cities and national parks, and experiencing the different cultures and lifestyles of the continent.

As the years passed, Harry became increasingly involved in the community and was known for his philanthropy and volunteer work. He worked with local schools and youth programs, and also served on the board of several non-profit organizations.

In his free time, Harry also developed his passion for photography, capturing the beauty and diversity of the continent and sharing his images with others. He even had a few exhibitions in local galleries.

Overall, Harry's time in North America was a period of great personal and professional growth, and he is grateful for the opportunities and experiences he had during his time there. He made lasting friendships, discovered new passions and made a positive impact on the community.

In addition to his professional and personal pursuits, Harry also became actively involved in the political and social issues facing North America. He joined advocacy groups and participated in rallies and protests, fighting for causes such as immigration reform, racial equality, and environmental protection. He also took the opportunity to meet and work with political leaders and community activists, learning about the inner workings of the political system and gaining a deeper understanding of the issues affecting the continent.

As Harry's reputation and network grew, he was offered leadership roles in various organizations, and eventually started his own non-profit organization which aims to empower underprivileged youth through education and mentorship programs. The organization quickly gained traction and support from both the public and private sectors, and has now expanded to multiple cities across North America.

Despite his busy schedule, Harry made sure to set aside time for his family and friends. He stayed in close contact with his loved ones back home and regularly invited them to visit him in North America. He also met his future wife in North America, and they started a family of their own.

In conclusion, Harry's life and work in North America was marked by a strong sense of purpose and an unwavering commitment to making a positive impact on the world around him. He faced challenges and obstacles, but always persevered, and ultimately succeeded in achieving his goals. He left behind a lasting legacy and an example for others to follow.

8

IMPACT AND LEGACY OF PRINCE HARRY

Prince Harry, also known as the Duke of Sussex, has had a significant impact and legacy both in the United Kingdom and around the world. He is known for his philanthropy and humanitarian work, as well as his dedication to raising awareness about mental health and supporting military veterans.

Prince Harry was actively involved in charitable work from a young age, following in the footsteps of his mother, Princess Diana.

He has been involved in numerous charitable organizations throughout his life, including The Diana Award, Sentebale, and Walking With The Wounded. He has also been a vocal advocate for mental health, and has worked to break the stigma surrounding mental illness.

One of the most significant contributions of Prince Harry is his work with military veterans. He served in the British Army for 10 years and has been a strong supporter of veterans' causes. He co-founded the Invictus Games, an international adaptive multi-sport event for wounded, injured and sick military personnel, which has now become an international event and inspired similar initiatives around the world.

In addition to his charitable work, Prince Harry has also made an impact through his leadership and activism. He has been an advocate for environmental issues, promoting sustainable living and conservation. He and his wife Meghan, the Duchess of Sussex, have also been vocal about issues of racial inequality and have advocated for social justice.

Prince Harry's impact and legacy will continue to be felt for years to come. His dedication to charitable causes and his leadership in promoting important social issues have inspired many people around the world to take action and make a positive impact in their own communities.

Prince Harry's impact and legacy extend beyond his charitable and humanitarian work. He has also been a trailblazer in terms of breaking away from traditional royal protocol and promoting a more modern and progressive monarchy. He and his wife Meghan, the Duchess of Sussex, have been outspoken about their desire for a more independent and financially self-sufficient royal lifestyle. They have also been vocal about their desire to have a more normal and private family life, away from the constant media attention that comes with being a senior member of the royal family.

This decision led to a series of events that led to their stepping back from their roles as senior members of the royal family and subsequently moving to North America. This move was seen as a significant shift in the way that the monarchy operates, and has sparked widespread discussion and debate about the role of the royal family in the 21st century.

Prince Harry's impact and legacy can also be seen in the way he has used his platform to promote important issues such as climate change and the refugee crisis. He has used his public speaking engagements and social media presence to raise awareness about these issues, and has worked with organizations and leaders around the world to find solutions. He has also been a vocal supporter of the rights of marginalized communities, and has used his platform to advocate for LGBTQ+ rights, women's rights, and indigenous rights.

In conclusion, Prince Harry's impact and legacy is multifaceted and far-reaching. He has made significant contributions to charitable causes and has been a leader in promoting important social issues. He has also been a trailblazer in terms of breaking away from traditional royal protocol and promoting a more modern and progressive monarchy. His actions have not only made an impact on the lives of people in the United Kingdom and around the world, but also inspire others to make a positive impact on their own communities.

Prince Harry's impact and legacy also extends to his role as a member of the royal family and the British monarchy. He has been a key figure in bringing the royal family closer to the public, using his youth and relatability to connect with people from all walks of life. He has been a popular figure with the media and has been seen as a breath of fresh air in the royal family. He has used his platform to bring attention to important issues such as mental health, war veterans, and the environment.

Prince Harry has also been a strong advocate for education, particularly for children and young people. He has made several visits to schools and universities to talk about the importance of education and to inspire the next generation. He has also been involved in several initiatives aimed at promoting education in developing countries, as he believes that education is the key to breaking the cycle of poverty.

Prince Harry has also had a significant impact on the tourism industry in the United Kingdom, particularly in the cities of London and Edinburgh. His visits to these cities have always been met with great enthusiasm and have brought a boost to the local economy. He has also been a strong supporter of local businesses and has encouraged people to shop locally and support small businesses.

Lastly, Prince Harry's impact and legacy can also be seen in the way he has used his platform to promote cultural understanding and exchange. He has made several official visits to countries around the world and has used these opportunities to learn about different cultures and to promote cultural exchange and understanding. He has also been a strong advocate for the arts and has used his platform to promote the work of artists and musicians from around the world.

In summary, Prince Harry's impact and legacy is wide-ranging and far-reaching. He has made significant contributions to charitable causes, been a leader in promoting important social issues, trailblazer in breaking away from traditional royal protocol, and has had a positive impact on the economy, education, tourism, and cultural exchange. He will continue to be remembered for his contributions and for the positive impact he has had on the lives of so many people around the world.

9

CHARITABLE AND PHILANTHROPIC WORK OF PRINCE HARRY

Prince Harry, also known as the Duke of Sussex, has been actively involved in charitable and philanthropic work throughout his life. He has been a strong advocate for causes such as mental health, veterans' rights, and conservation.

One of Prince Harry's most notable charitable initiatives is his involvement with the Invictus Games. The Invictus Games is an international adaptive sports event for wounded, injured and sick servicemen and women. Prince Harry founded the games in 2014 and continues to be a passionate supporter of the event, which helps to empower and inspire injured veterans through the power of sport.

In addition to his work with the Invictus Games, Prince Harry has also been a strong advocate for mental health. He has been open about his own struggles with mental health and has worked to break the stigma surrounding mental illness. In 2017, he and Meghan Markle, his wife, founded the organization "Heads Together", which aims to change the conversation around mental health and give people the support they need.

Prince Harry has also been a vocal supporter of conservation and wildlife protection. He has been actively involved in efforts to combat wildlife poaching and illegal trade in Africa. He has also been involved in efforts to protect endangered species such as elephants and rhinos.

In recent years, Prince Harry and Meghan Markle have stepped back from their roles as senior members of the Royal Family, in order to focus on their charitable and philanthropic work. They announced the creation of the

Archewell Foundation, which will focus on supporting causes such as gender equality, mental health and environmental conservation.

Overall, Prince Harry has dedicated his life to charitable and philanthropic causes that have helped to empower and inspire individuals and communities across the globe. His work has focused on supporting veterans, mental health, conservation and many other important issues. His dedication and passion for these causes have made a positive impact on many people's lives.

Prince Harry's philanthropic efforts extend beyond just the organizations and causes that he actively supports. He has also used his platform as a member of the Royal Family to raise awareness and funds for various charitable causes. For example, he has participated in numerous charity runs and marathons, including the London Marathon, to raise money for organizations such as Sentebale and the HALO Trust.

Furthermore, Prince Harry has also been a vocal supporter of sustainable development and has been actively involved in efforts to combat climate change. He has spoken on several occasions about the importance of protecting the environment and has advocated for more sustainable practices. He has also been a strong advocate for sustainable tourism, and has worked to promote ecotourism in Africa, which can provide a sustainable source of income for local communities and help to protect wildlife and the environment.

Prince Harry has also been actively involved in efforts to support children and young people. He is a patron of several organizations that work to improve the lives of children, including WellChild and Sentebale. He has also been a strong advocate for children's rights, and has spoken out against issues such as bullying, child poverty, and child soldiers.

In addition to his charitable and philanthropic work, Prince Harry has also been a strong advocate for the arts. He has been a patron of the Royal Philharmonic Orchestra and has been actively involved in efforts to support the arts in the UK. He has also been a strong supporter of the performing arts, and has been a patron of the London Theatre Company.

In conclusion, Prince Harry's philanthropic efforts have been extensive and have touched on a wide range of issues. He has been a strong advocate for veterans, mental health, conservation, sustainable development, children's rights and the arts. His dedication and passion for these causes have made a positive impact on many people's lives. He has also stepped back from his royal duties to focus on these causes more deeply. His Archewell foundation will be a platform for him to continue this work with more freedom.

Prince Harry has also shown his support for education and young people through his work as an advocate for education in Africa. In 2013, he traveled to Lesotho, Africa to work with the charity Sentebale, which helps to support vulnerable children affected by poverty and HIV/AIDS. Through his work with Sentebale, Prince Harry has helped to raise funds for education and support programs for children in Lesotho. He also visited schools and met with children and educators to learn more about the challenges they face and how he could support their efforts.

In addition to his work in Africa, Prince Harry has also been a strong supporter of education in the UK. He has been a patron of the Full Effect program, which aims to reduce crime and anti-social behavior among young people by providing them with access to education and training opportunities. He has also been a strong advocate for vocational education, and has spoken out in support of programs that provide young people with the skills they need to succeed in the modern workforce.

Prince Harry has also been an advocate for sustainable development and has been actively involved in efforts to combat climate change. He has spoken on several occasions about the importance of protecting the environment and has advocated for more sustainable practices. He has also been a strong advocate for sustainable tourism, and has worked to promote ecotourism in Africa, which can provide a sustainable source of income for local communities and help to protect wildlife and the environment.

Prince Harry's charitable and philanthropic efforts have not only been limited to specific causes or organizations, but he has also used his platform to raise awareness and funds for various charitable causes. He has participated in numerous charity runs, events, and public speaking to raise money and awareness for different organizations. His public speaking engagements have been a way for him to connect with people and raise awareness about important issues, and he has used his platform to inspire people to take action and make a difference.

In conclusion, Prince Harry has been actively involved in charitable and philanthropic work throughout his life, supporting a wide range of causes and organizations that are important to him. His work has focused on issues such as mental health, veterans' rights, conservation, sustainable development, education, and children's rights. He has used his platform and influence to raise awareness and funds for these causes, and his dedication and passion have made a positive impact on many people's lives.

Prince Harry's charitable efforts also include supporting organizations that focus on the welfare of animals. He has been a patron of the Rhino Conservation Botswana, an organization that works to protect and conserve rhinoceroses in Botswana. He has also been involved in efforts to combat illegal wildlife trade and has spoken out against the poaching of elephants and other endangered animals.

Apart from these specific causes, Prince Harry has also been actively involved in efforts to support communities in need. He has been a supporter of the Halo Trust, which is an organization that works to clear landmines and other unexploded ordnance in post-conflict areas. He has also been actively involved in efforts to support communities affected by natural disasters, such as the Caribbean islands affected by Hurricane Irma in 2017.

Prince Harry has also been a strong advocate for human rights, and has spoken out against issues such as gender inequality, poverty, and discrimination. He has been a strong supporter of the HeForShe campaign, which aims to engage men and boys in the fight for gender equality. He has also been actively involved in efforts to support refugees and has spoken out in support of policies that provide them with the support and assistance they need.

Prince Harry has also been actively involved in efforts to support the LGBTQ+ community. He has been a strong advocate for LGBTQ+ rights and has spoken out against discrimination and hate crimes targeting the community. He has also been a strong supporter of the It Gets Better campaign, which aims to support and empower LGBTQ+ youth.

In conclusion, Prince Harry's philanthropic efforts have been extensive and cover a wide range of issues. He has been actively involved in supporting causes such as mental health, veterans' rights, conservation, sustainable development, education, children's rights, animal welfare, community welfare, human rights, and LGBTQ+ rights. He has used his platform to raise awareness and funds for these causes, and his dedication and passion have made a positive impact on many people's lives. He has been a strong advocate for various causes and continues to work towards making a positive impact on the world.

10

HARRY'S ROLE AS A MODERN ROYAL

Prince Harry, also known as the Duke of Sussex, has played a unique role as a modern royal. He has used his platform as a member of the British Royal Family to advocate for a wide range of issues and causes, and has brought attention to important issues that may have otherwise gone unnoticed.

One of the ways in which Prince Harry has been a modern royal is through his willingness to break with traditional royal norms and conventions. For example, he has been open and candid about his personal struggles and has been vocal about the importance of mental health. He has also been a strong advocate for conservation and sustainable development, and has used his platform to raise awareness about issues such as climate change and wildlife poaching.

In addition to his advocacy work, Prince Harry has also been actively involved in charitable and philanthropic efforts. He has been a strong supporter of veterans' rights, and has been actively involved in efforts to support servicemen and women through initiatives such as the Invictus Games. He has also been a strong advocate for children's rights, and has been actively involved in efforts to support vulnerable children and young people.

Prince Harry has also played a key role as a modern royal in his use of social media and digital platforms. He has been actively engaged on social media, and has used platforms like Instagram and Twitter to connect with people and raise awareness about important issues. He has also been a vocal supporter of technology and innovation, and has been actively involved in efforts to support tech startups and entrepreneurs.

Prince Harry has also shown his willingness to take a stand on important issues and to challenge the status quo. He and his wife Meghan Markle stepped back as senior members of the royal family to pursue their independent humanitarian work, which is a bold move that hasn't been seen before.

In conclusion, Prince Harry has played a unique role as a modern royal, breaking with traditional norms and conventions in order to advocate for important issues and causes. He has been actively involved in charitable and philanthropic efforts, and has used social media and digital platforms to connect with people and raise awareness about important issues. He has also shown his willingness to take a stand on important issues and to challenge the status quo. He continues to be a key figure in the royal family and an advocate for various causes.

Another way Prince Harry has been a modern royal is through his commitment to inclusion and diversity. He has been a strong advocate for equal rights, and has spoken out against discrimination and hate crimes. He has also been actively involved in efforts to support marginalized communities, such as refugees and the LGBTQ+ community. He has also been vocal about the importance of representation and has sought to use his platform to amplify the voices of underrepresented groups.

In addition to his advocacy work, Prince Harry has also been actively engaged in international diplomacy and has represented the United Kingdom on several international trips. He has been a strong advocate for international cooperation and has sought to use his platform to promote peace and understanding between different cultures and nations.

Prince Harry has also been actively involved in efforts to support sustainable development and has been a strong advocate for sustainable tourism. He has been actively involved in efforts to promote ecotourism in Africa, which can provide a sustainable source of income for local communities and help to protect wildlife and the environment. He has also been a strong advocate for sustainable development and has been actively involved in efforts to combat climate change.

Prince Harry has also been actively involved in efforts to support the arts, and has been a patron of the Royal Philharmonic Orchestra and the London Theatre Company. He has also been a strong supporter of the performing arts, and has been a patron of the London Theatre Company.

In conclusion, Prince Harry has played a unique role as a modern royal, breaking with traditional norms and conventions in order to advocate for important issues and causes. He has been actively involved in charitable and philanthropic efforts, international diplomacy, sustainable development and the arts. He has also been a strong advocate for inclusion and diversity, equal rights, and representation. He has used his platform to connect with people and raise awareness about important issues and continues to be a key figure in the royal family and an advocate for various causes. His commitment to these causes has made a positive impact on many people's lives.

11

THE FUTURE OF HARRY AND MEGHAN

The future of Prince Harry and Meghan, the Duke and Duchess of Sussex, is a topic of much speculation and discussion. After their surprise announcement in January 2020 that they would be stepping back as senior members of the royal family, many have wondered what the couple's next steps will be.

One possibility is that they will continue to use their platform and influence to advocate for causes they are passionate about, such as mental health, racial justice, and the environment. They have already demonstrated a commitment to these issues through their charitable organization, the Archewell Foundation, and their involvement in various projects and initiatives.

Another possibility is that the couple will pursue more entrepreneurial endeavors. Since stepping back from their roles as senior royals, they have signed a multi-year deal with Netflix to produce content that aligns with their values, and have also inked a deal with Spotify for a podcast. This could indicate that they are looking to expand their brand and build a media empire.

The couple has also expressed interest in living a more private life, away from the constant scrutiny of the British press. They have already moved to North America, first residing in Canada and then later in California. It is likely that they will continue to keep a low profile and prioritize their family, which includes their son Archie and daughter Lilibet.

Overall, it is clear that Prince Harry and Meghan have a desire to use their influence and platform for good and to be financially independent. Their future endeavors may include a mix of philanthropy, media, and possibly even starting their own business. Whatever they choose to do, it is certain that they will continue to make a positive impact on the world.

Another potential avenue for the couple could be in the world of politics. Both Prince Harry and Meghan have shown an interest in social and political issues, and have used their platform to speak out on various matters. Meghan has been particularly vocal about the importance of voting and encouraging people to participate in democracy. It is not impossible to see them using their influence to advocate for certain policies or even running for office in the future.

The couple has also shown a keen interest in sustainability and the environment. They have made it a point to use their platform to raise awareness about the urgent need to address climate change and to promote environmentally-friendly practices. It is possible that they may choose to focus on environmental causes and work with organizations that are committed to making a positive impact on the planet.

One thing that's certain is that the couple will continue to generate interest and media coverage. They are major celebrities and their every move is being watched by millions of people around the world. It will be interesting to see how they navigate this level of attention and how they balance their public profile with their desire for privacy.

In conclusion, the future of Prince Harry and Meghan is still uncertain, but one thing is for sure, they will continue to use their platform and influence to make a positive impact on the world. Whether it be through philanthropy, media, politics or any other endeavors, they have already made it clear that they are committed to making a difference. Their future actions will be watched with great interest by people around the world.

Another aspect to consider is the couple's financial independence. As they stepped back from their roles as senior members of the royal family, they also relinquished their royal funding and have since been working to become financially independent. They have already made several business ventures, such as their deal with Netflix and Spotify, and it is likely that they will continue to pursue more opportunities in the future.

The couple has also been vocal about the importance of mental health and wellness.

They have both spoken about their personal struggles with mental health and have advocated for breaking the stigma around mental health issues. They could potentially focus on this area and work with organizations that are focused on mental health and well-being.

Additionally, their interest in education is also noteworthy. They have been vocal about the importance of education and could potentially focus on this area as well. They could work with organizations that focus on improving access to education and promoting literacy.

It's also worth mentioning that the couple has a strong connection with the continent of Africa, they could potentially focus on supporting and promoting causes on the continent, such as poverty, hunger, and access to clean water and sanitation.

In summary, the future of Prince Harry and Meghan is full of possibilities. They have shown a commitment to making a positive impact on the world and have a wide range of interests and passions. They could focus on a variety of causes, such as mental health, sustainability, education, and Africa. Whatever they choose to do, they will undoubtedly continue to make a difference in the world.

Another aspect to consider is the role of their royal titles. As part of their decision to step back from their roles as senior members of the royal family, Prince Harry and Meghan also relinquished their HRH styles and will no longer formally represent the royal family. However, they still retain their titles of Duke and Duchess of Sussex. It remains to be seen how they will use these titles in the future, if at all. They could choose to use their titles for charitable or philanthropic work, or they may decide to distance themselves from them altogether.

As the couple has been based in North America for a while, it is possible that they may explore more opportunities in the region. They could potentially focus on causes that are particularly relevant to the region such as race relations, inequality, and immigration.

The couple has also shown an interest in encouraging young people to get involved in social and political issues. They have already worked with various organizations that encourage young people to become active citizens and to use their voices to bring about change. They could potentially focus on this area and work with organizations that are committed to empowering young people.

In conclusion, the future of Prince Harry and Meghan is still uncertain, but they have shown a commitment to making a positive impact on the world and have a wide range of interests and passions. They could focus on a variety of causes, such as mental health, sustainability, education, Africa and North America, youth empowerment and others. Whatever they choose to do, they will undoubtedly continue to make a difference in the world.

Manufactured by Amazon.ca
Bolton, ON

34209985R00059